BETTER BOOK REPORTS

by
Joanne Richards & Marianne Standley

Incentive Publications, Inc.
Nashville, Tennessee

Cover by Susan Harrison
Edited by Sally Sharpe

ISBN 0-86530-102-6

Table of Contents

INTRODUCTION

BETTER BOOK REPORTS is a collection of unique ideas designed to help students turn traditional book reporting into a creative expression writing adventure!

This book offers a new approach to ordinary book reporting. By completing miniature "books," students will experience the success of self-expression and the excitement of creativity as they discover and share the world of reading.

All of the necessary booklet patterns and writing "stimulators" are included. Simply reproduce the appropriate pages in quantities to meet the needs of the class and guide the students by giving basic instructions for the assembly of the booklets. Students will be proud of their accomplishments and will develop a "thirst" for reading as they enjoy producing "better book reports"!

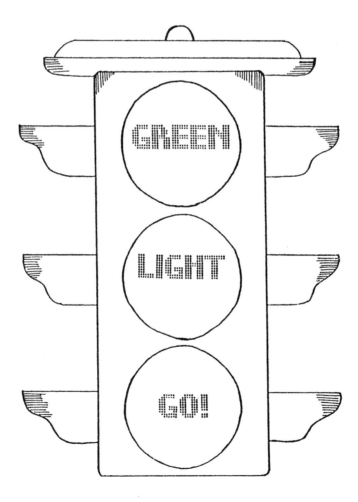

_____ puts_____in
apple pie order.

Apple Pie Order

Are your students' book reports "going to seed"? Help students get to the "core" of writing sequential events with this project that will become the "apple of your eye"!

DIRECTIONS

1. Reproduce the cover page and lined apple page (pages 7 and 8) in quantities to meet the needs of the class. (The number of lined pages each student needs will vary.)

2. Reproduce page 10 for each student. Instruct the students to use any or all of the context clues to sequence the events or explain the characters of the chosen book.

3. Have the students "cut out" the pages following the apple design and assemble the pages in the desired order with the cover sheet on top. The students may punch holes in the pages and tie them together with yarn.

4. Instruct each student to write the author's name or his or her own name on the first line of the cover sheet and the title of the book on the second line.

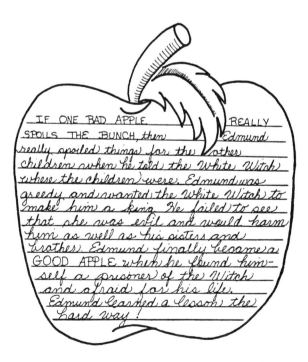

CONTEXT CLUES

1. The events of _____ by _____ are in "apple pie order"! (Student sequences the events of the book.)

2. _____ really "went to seed" when _____ .

3. If "one bad apple spoils the bunch," then _____ spoiled things for _____ when _____ .

4. _____ upset _____ 's "apple cart" when _____ .

5. _____ was the "apple of _____ 's eye" when _____ .

6. _____ was an "apple polisher" the time that _____ .

7. The "core" of _____ 's problems was _____ .

8. All of _____ 's problems seemed to "stem" from _____ .

9. _____ "tried to worm his/her way out of" _____ .

10. _____ "hid his/her light under a bushel" because _____ .

11. I recommend _____ to other " bookworms" because _____.

12. The character with the most "a-peel" was _____ because _____ .

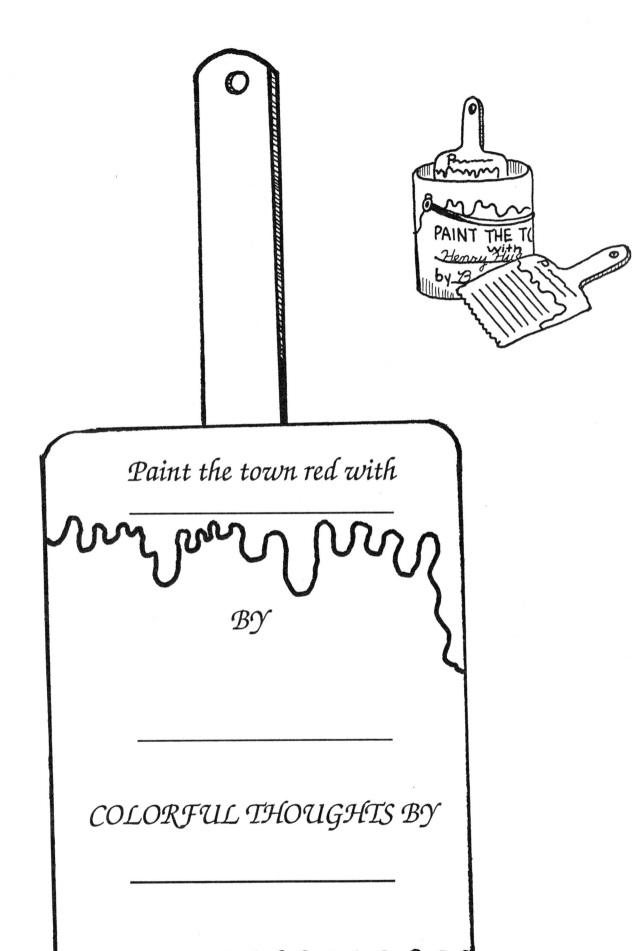

Paint the town red with

_____

BY

_____

COLORFUL THOUGHTS BY

_____

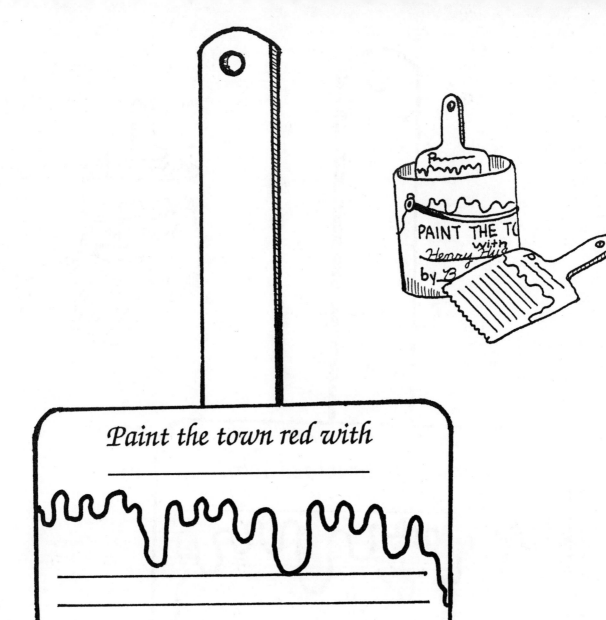

Paint the town red with

_____

Give dull book reporting the "brush off"! Help students "brighten" their reading experiences with this activity that shows how book characters "painted the town red"!

DIRECTIONS

1. Reproduce the cover page and lined paintbrush page (pages 11 and 12) in quantities to meet the needs of the class. (Each student will need a lined page for every character in the chosen book.)

2. Instruct the students to write a character's name at the top of each lined page and to write about what the character does for amusement or entertainment.

3. Have the students "cut out" the pages following the paintbrush design and assemble the pages in the desired order with the cover sheet on top. The students may punch holes in the pages and tie them together with yarn.

4. Instruct each student to write the book title on the first line of the cover sheet, the author's name on the second line, and his or her own name on the third line.

SUGGESTED DISPLAY

1. Cover a large coffee can with foil.

2. Make two holes on either side of the can near the top.

3. Hook the ends of a 14-inch wire through the holes to make a handle.

4. Use a bright color of construction paper to make a "paint spill." Glue the spill to the top edge of the can so that it appears to be "pouring out" of the can.

5. Place the students' paintbrush booklets in the can for display.

Paint the Town Red!

DeLIGHTful

is turned on by

by

"Light up" book reporting with this electrifying idea that's bound to "turn on" your students! Books with characters who have "bright ideas" or who "shed light" on situations in the book are perfect selections for this project.

DIRECTIONS

1. Reproduce the cover page and lined light bulb page (pages 15 and 16) in quantities to meet the needs of the class. (The number of lined pages each student needs will vary.)

2. Reproduce page 18 for each student. Instruct the students to use any or all of the context clues to explain how book characters use bright ideas to solve problems or to show how characters shed light on situations in the book.

3. Have the students "cut out" the pages following the light bulb design and assemble the pages in the desired order with the cover page on top. The students may punch holes in the pages and tie them together with yarn.

4. Instruct each student to write his or her name on the first line of the cover page, the title of the book on the second line, and the author's name on the third line.

CONTEXT CLUES

1. _____ is a "deLIGHTful" character in this book because _____ .

2. _____ 's face "lit up" whenever _____ .

3. All of _____ 's ideas were "plugged" into _____ the time that _____ .

4. _____ had the "bright idea" to _____ when _____ .

5. _____ 's "electric personality" was shown by _____ .

6. _____ finally "saw the light" after _____ .

7. _____ "switched on" to _____ after _____ .

8. _____ received "glowing reports" about _____ .

SUNNY SIDE UP

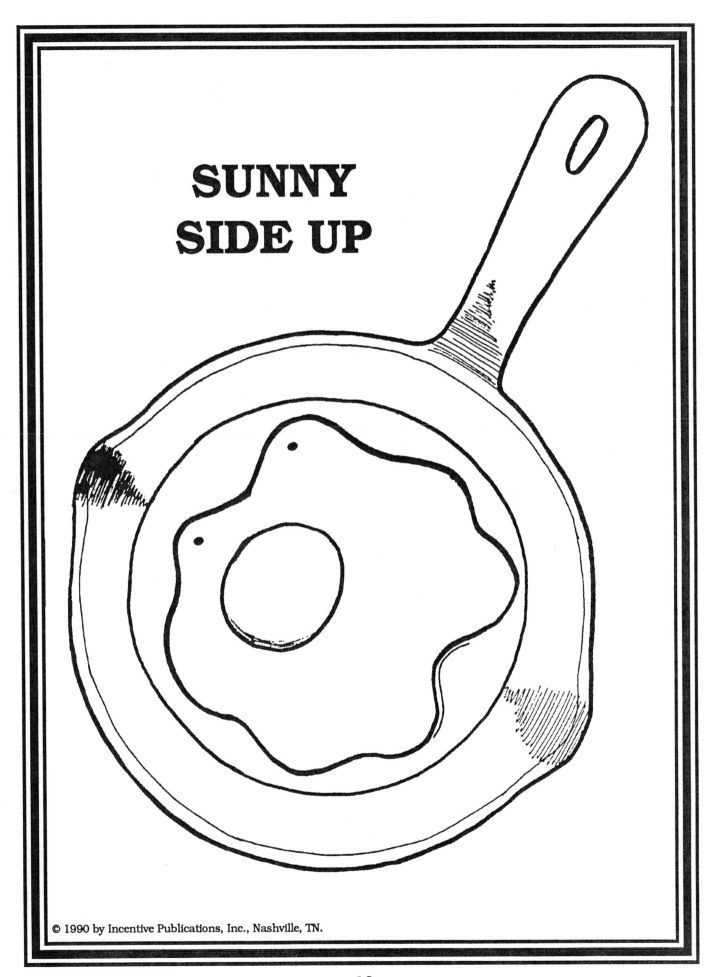

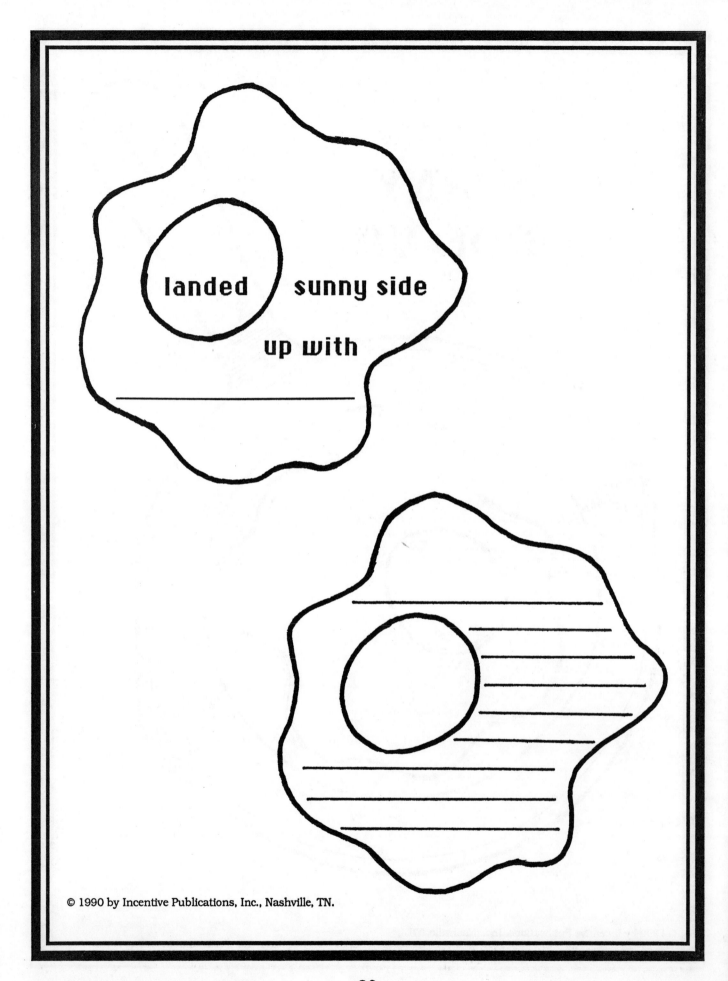

landed sunny side up with

_____

Take book reporting "off the back burner"! This grade A idea is perfect for writing about happy endings.

DIRECTIONS

1. Reproduce the frying pan and egg patterns (pages 19 and 20) in quantities to meet the needs of the class. (The number of lined pages that each student needs will vary.)

2. Have each student cut and paste one "cover page" egg on a frying pan to make a cover page and several lined eggs on frying pans to make booklet pages.

3. Reproduce page 22 for each student. Instruct the students to use any or all of the context clues to explain how book characters "end up" in happy situations.

4. Have the students "cut out" the pages following the frying pan design and assemble the pages in the desired order with the cover page on top. The students may punch holes in the frying pan handles and loop yarn, ribbon, or string through the holes to tie the pages together.

5. Instruct each student to write his or her name on the first line of the cover page and the title of the book on the second line.

6. Hang the booklets in the room for display.

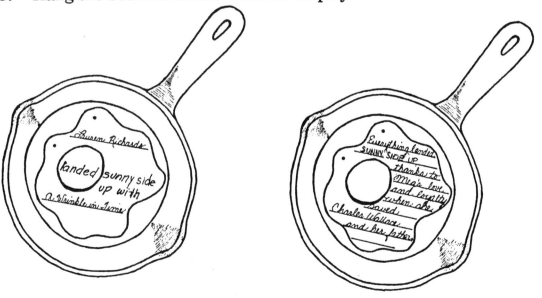

CONTEXT CLUES

1. _____ was an "eggs-pert" at
_____ .

2. _____ really "laid an egg" the time that
_____ .

3. _____ learned not to "put all his/her eggs in one
basket" after _____ .

4. _____ was a "rotten egg" because
_____ .

5. _____ 's thoughts became "scrambled" whenever
_____ .

6. _____ was "eggs-tra special" to _____
every time that _____ .

7. _____ caused _____ to "come out
of his/her shell" when _____ .

8. Everything landed "sunny side up" thanks to
_____ .

9. _____ was a "grade A" character because
_____ .

Reflections

_____

Looked Into

_____

By

_____

Your students can improve their book reporting "images" with this "eye-opening" idea! This activity is designed for books with characters who change their images or who are forced to reflect upon their actions or situations.

DIRECTIONS

1. Reproduce the cover page and lined mirror page (pages 23 and 24) in quantities to meet the needs of the class. (The number of lined pages each student needs will vary.)

2. Reproduce page 26 for each student. Instruct the students to use any or all of the context clues to explain how the characters in the chosen book reflect upon their actions or situations or how they change their images.

3. Have the students "cut out" the pages following the mirror design and assemble the pages in the desired order with the cover page on top. The students may punch holes in the pages and tie them together with yarn.

4. Instruct each student to write his or her name on the first line of the cover page, the book title on the second line, and the author's name on the third line.

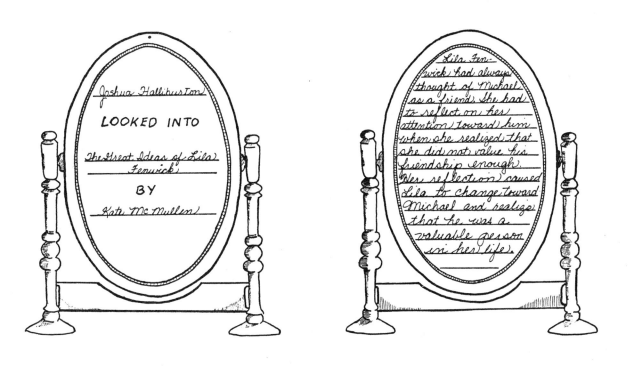

CONTEXT CLUES

1. _____ "looked at the world through rose-colored glasses" after _____ .

2. _____ "looked forward to" _____ when _____ .

3. _____ 's "image" was _____ after _____ .

4. _____ "reflected" on _____ and decided to _____ .

5. _____ looked _____ "in the eye" and _____ .

6. _____ "saw it fit" to _____ when _____ .

7. _____ "saw eye to eye" with _____ about _____ .

8. "At first glance," _____ thought _____ , but later he/she decided that _____ .

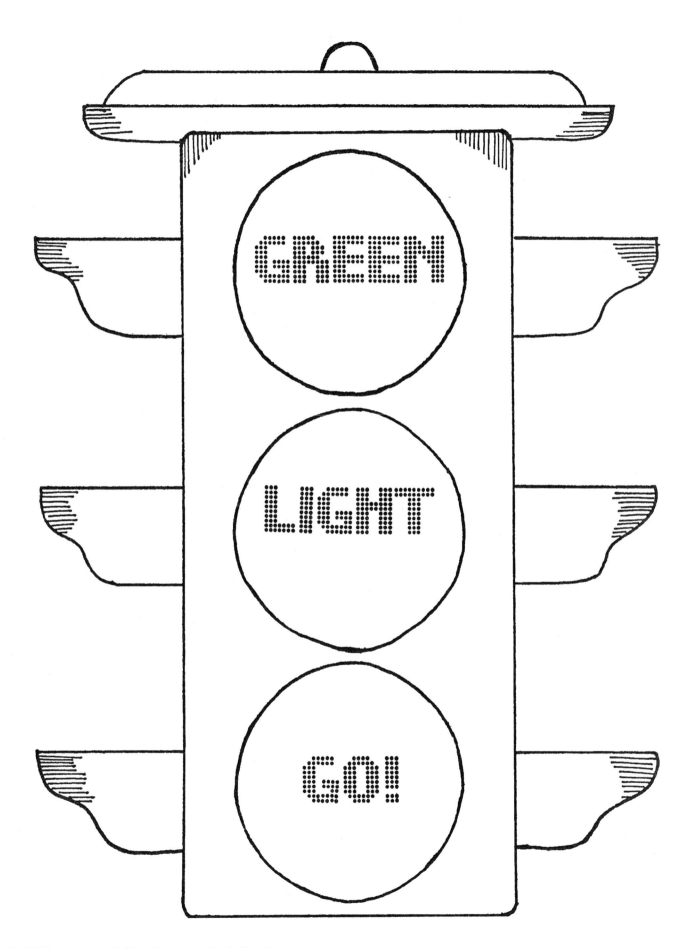

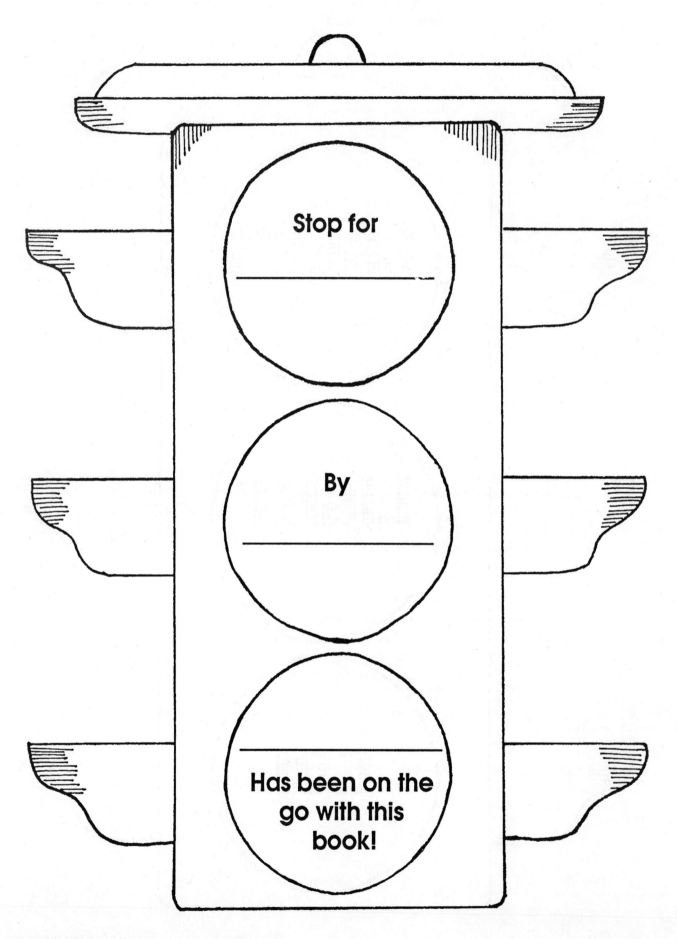

Stop for

_____

By

_____

_____

Has been on the
go with this
book!

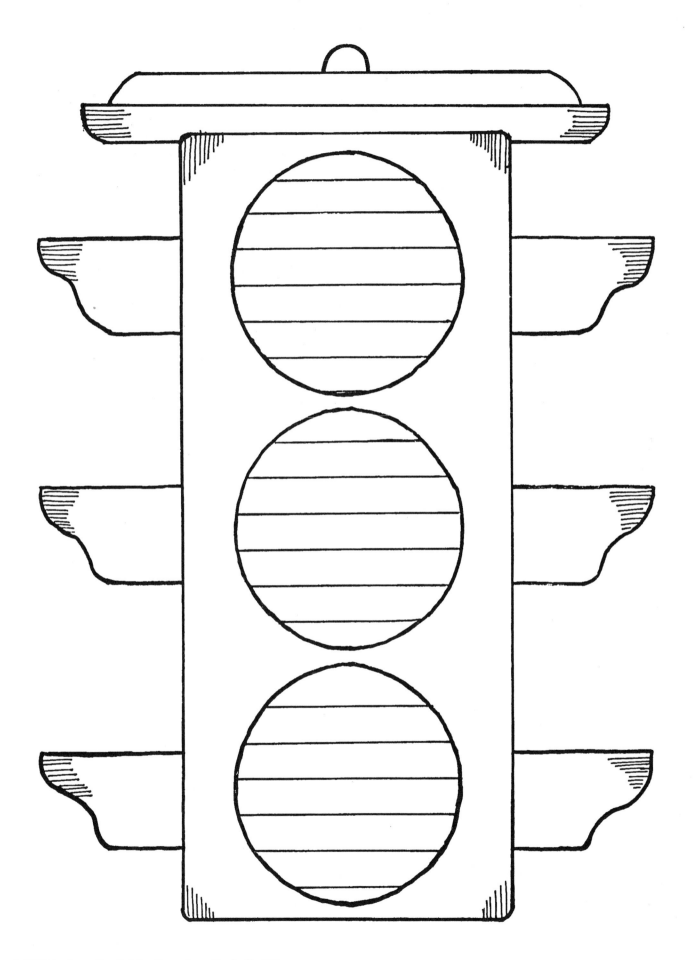

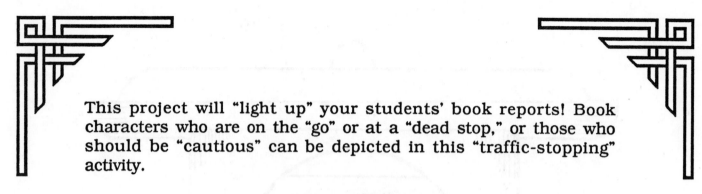

This project will "light up" your students' book reports! Book characters who are on the "go" or at a "dead stop," or those who should be "cautious" can be depicted in this "traffic-stopping" activity.

DIRECTIONS

1. Reproduce the traffic light pattern on pages 27-29 in quantities to meet the needs of the class. (Each student will need a lined page for each main character in the chosen book.)

2. Instruct each student to write the following on a lined traffic light page:

   • top light — tell how the character came to a stop
   • middle light — tell how the character needed to be cautious
   • bottom light — tell how the character was "on the move"

3. Have each student write the book title on the first line of page 28, the author's name on the second line, and his or her own name on the bottom line.

4. Have the students "cut out" the pages following the traffic light design and assemble the pages in the desired order with pages 27 and 28 on top (in that order). The students may punch holes in the pages and tie them together with yarn.

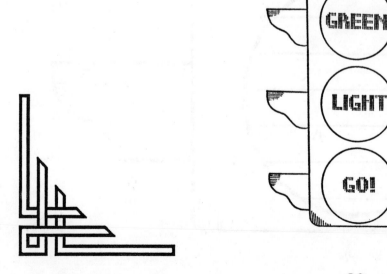

Timely Thoughts
from

_____

by

_____

Timekeeper

_____

THE TIME IS
NOW!

THE TIME IS
NOW!

...Just in the nick of time! Here's a book project that's guaranteed to give your students "hours" of fun!

DIRECTIONS

1. Reproduce the cover page and lined hourglass page (pages 31 and 32) in quantities to meet the needs of the class. (The number of lined pages each student needs will vary.)

2. Reproduce page 34 for each student. Instruct the students to use any or all of the context clues to explain the actions or events in the chosen book.

3. Have the students "cut out" the pages following the hourglass design and assemble the pages in the desired order with the cover page on top. The students may punch holes in the pages and tie them together with yarn.

4. Instruct each student to write the book title on the first line of the cover page, the author's name on the second line, and his or her own name on the third line.

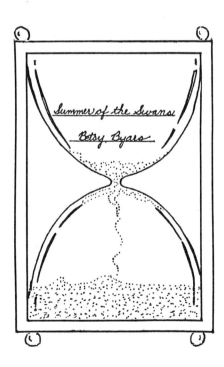

CONTEXT CLUES

1. _____ felt like he/she was "living on borrowed time" because _____ .

2. _____ "bided his/her time" so that he/she could _____ .

3. _____ "had the time of his/her life" when _____ .

4. "The time was ripe" for _____ to _____ when _____ .

5. "Time and time again," _____ _____ .

6. "The sands of time" seemed to _____.

7. "It was about time" that _____ _____ because _____ .

8. _____ gave _____ "a hard time" when _____ .

Timely Thoughts
from
Summer of the Swans
by
Betsy Byars

Timekeeper
Harriet A. Richards
The Time Is
NOW!

Sarah FELT LIKE SHE WAS LIVING ON BORROWED TIME _because she knew she must find her little brother soon after he wandered away and became lost._

The Time Is
NOW!

© 1990 by Incentive Publications, Inc., Nashville, TN.

JUST DESSERTS

Reading

_____

By

_____

Was a Piece of Cake for

_____

Put the "icing on the cake" with this creative book report project!

DIRECTIONS

1. Reproduce the cover page and lined cake page (pages 35 and 36) in quantities to meet the needs of the class. (The number of lined pages each student needs will vary.)

2. Reproduce page 38 for each student. Instruct the students to use any or all of the context clues to explain how characters in the chosen book are able to overcome their fears.

3. Have the students "cut out" the pages following the cake design and assemble them in the desired order with the cover page on top. The students may punch holes in the pages and tie them together with yarn.

4. Instruct each student to write the book title on the first line of the cover page, the author's name on the second line, and his or her own name on the third line.

CONTEXT CLUES

1. _____ tried to "have his/her cake and eat it too" when _____ .

2. _____ was the "icing on the cake" for _____ .

3. _____ tried to "sweet talk" _____ out of _____ .

4. _____ got his/her "just desserts" when _____ .

5. It was a "piece of cake" when _____ tried to _____ .

6. _____'s answer to _____ was "short and sweet" about _____ .

7. _____ acted like a "sweetie pie" about _____ .

8. No matter how you "slice" it, _____ acted _____ .

Prickly
Problems

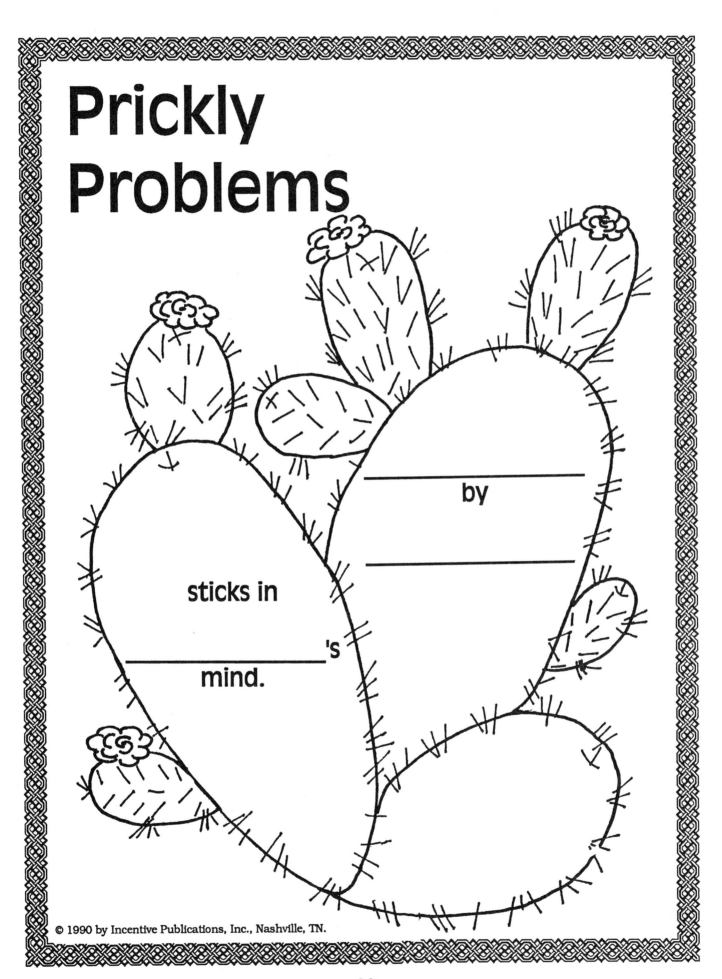

_____ by
_____

sticks in
_____'s
mind.

Here's a "sharp" idea to get your students "stuck" on book reporting! Use this project to describe characters who find themselves in difficult situations or who have "prickly" dispositions.

DIRECTIONS

1. Reproduce the cover page and lined cactus page (pages 39 and 40) in quantities to meet the needs of the class. (The number of lined pages each student needs will vary.)

2. Reproduce page 42 for each student. Instruct the students to use any or all of the context clues to describe how the characters in the chosen book get into and out of "prickly" situations, or how characters display "prickly" dispositions.

3. Have the students "cut out" the pages following the cactus design and assemble the pages in the desired order with the cover page on top. Students may punch holes in the pages and tie them together with yarn.

4. Instruct each student to write the book title on the first line of the cover page, the author's name on the second line, and his or her own name on the third line.

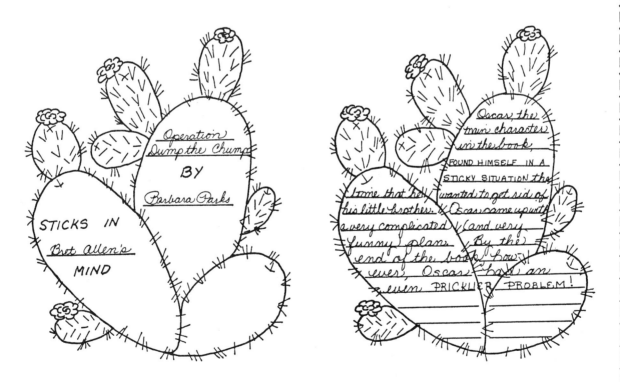

CONTEXT CLUES

1. _____ found himself/herself in a "sticky situation" the time that _____ .

2. _____ and _____ needed to "stick together" because _____ .

3. _____ decided to "stick around" _____ because _____ .

4. _____ "stuck" in _____ 's mind because _____ .

5. _____ seemed to have a "prickly" disposition when he/she _____ .

6. Home (school) was a "desert" to _____ because _____ .

7. Everyone thought that _____ was a "stick-in-the-mud" since _____ .

8. Everyone "needled" _____ when _____ .

TO THE RESCUE

_____

By

_____

Read by

_____ ,

Knight Errant

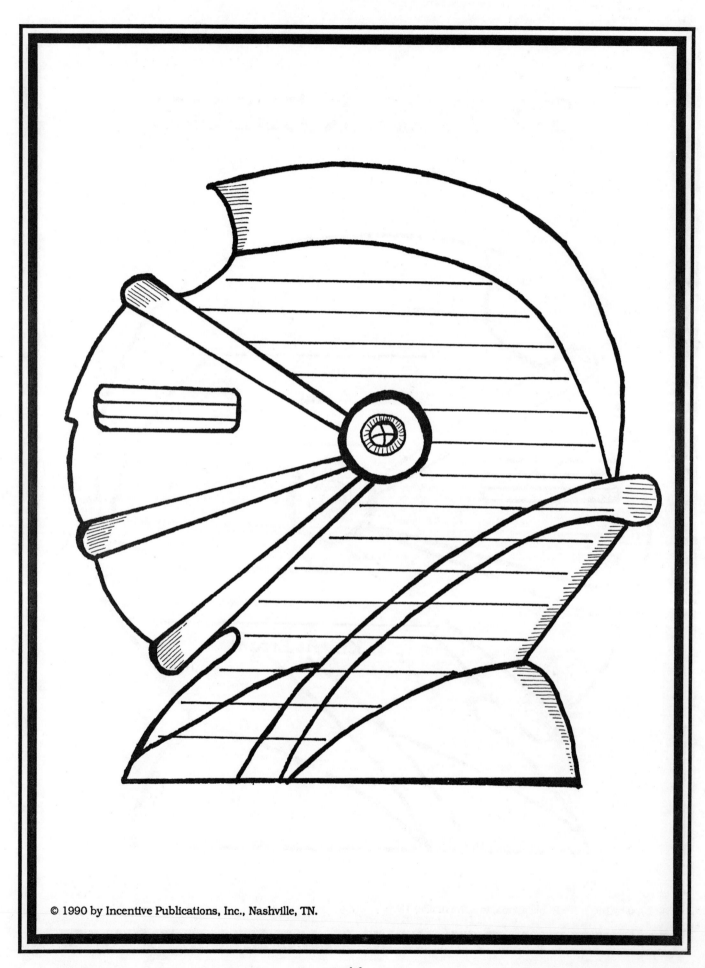

Your students will become "courageous" in their book reporting with this idea that "slays the dragon" of boredom!

DIRECTIONS

1. Reproduce the cover page and lined helmet page (pages 43 and 44) in quantities to meet the needs of the class. (The number of lined pages each student needs will vary.)

2. Reproduce page 46 for each student. Instruct the students to use any or all of the context clues to explain how book characters come to the rescue of other characters or arm themselves against adversity.

3. Have the students "cut out" the pages following the helmet design and assemble the pages in the desired order with the cover page on top. The students may punch holes in the pages and tie them together with yarn.

4. Instruct each student to write the book title on the first line of the cover page, the author's name on the second line, and his or her own name on the third line.

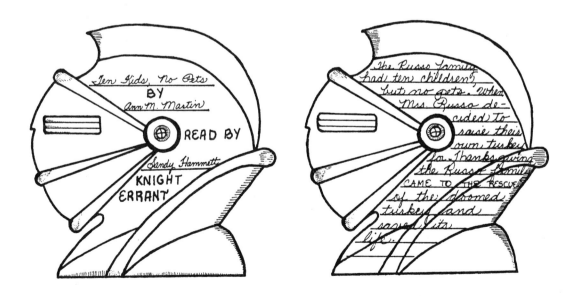

CONTEXT CLUES

1. _____ felt like a "knight in shining armor" whenever _____ .

2. _____ was "armed" for _____ the time that _____ .

3. _____ came to _____'s "rescue" when _____ .

4. _____ "battled it out" with _____ over _____ .

5. _____ "mustered up the courage" to _____ .

6. _____ had a "round-table discussion" with _____ about _____ .

7. _____ "slew the dragon" of _____ the time that _____ .

8. _____ "threw down the gauntlet" to _____ after _____ .

UNDER LOCK AND KEY

was locked into

by

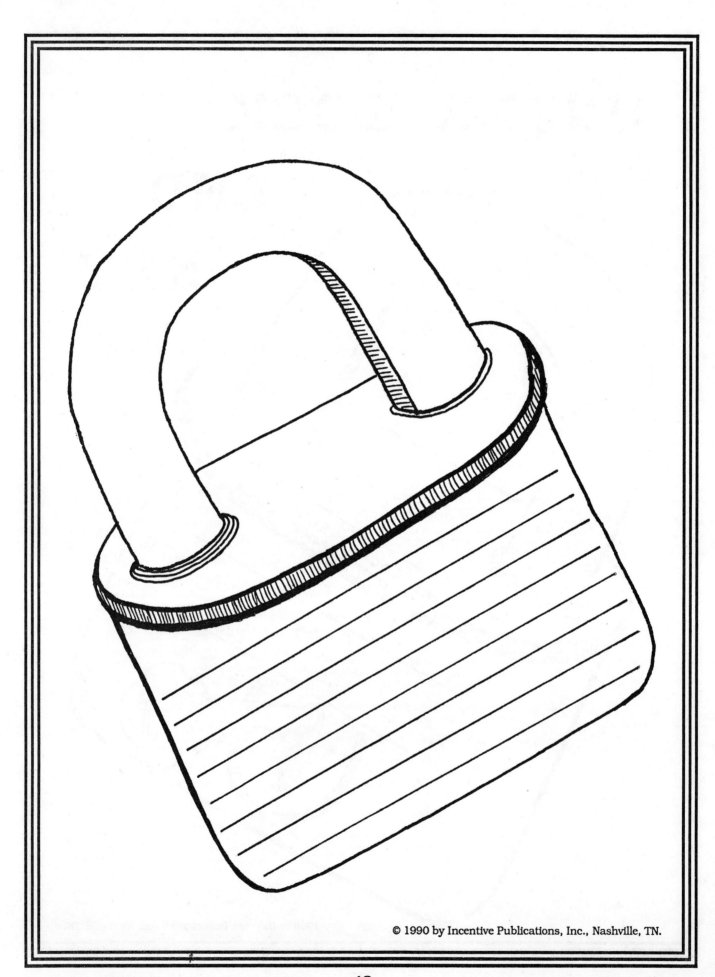

Are your students "locked in" to boring book reports? Help them find the right "combination" with this "key" idea! This project is perfect for books with characters who keep their feelings "locked up" or who feel "locked into" situations.

DIRECTIONS

1. Reproduce the cover page and lined book page (pages 47 and 48) in quantities to meet the needs of the class. (The number of lined pages each student needs will vary.)

2. Reproduce page 50 for each student. Instruct the students to use any or all of the context clues to describe how characters from the chosen book keep their feelings "locked" inside themselves and how they find the "keys" to their problems.

3. Have the students "cut out" the pages following the lock design and assemble the pages in the desired order with the cover page on top. The students may punch holes in the pages and tie them together with yarn.

4. Instruct each student to write his or her name on the first line of the cover page, the book title on the second line, and the author's name on the third line.

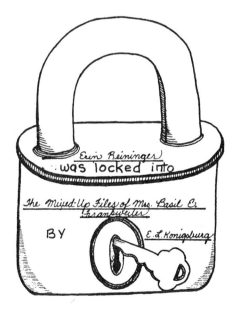
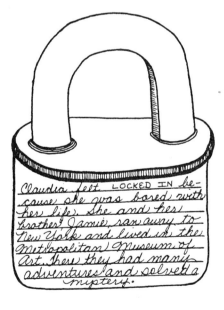

CONTEXT CLUES

1. _____ felt "locked in" because
   _____ .

2. The "combinations" of _____ ,
   _____ , and _____ made
   _____ feel _____ .

3. The "key" to _____ 's success/downfall
   was _____ . This led to _____ .

4. _____ felt very "secure"
   when _____ .

5. Everything "opened up" for _____ when
   _____ .

6. _____ got a "lock" on
   _____ after _____ .

7. _____ was a "safe" situation for
   _____ because _____ .

8. _____ "protected" _____ .
   An example of this is _____ .

IN A JAM

_____

THINKS

_____

BY

_____

IS A
BERRY GOOD BOOK!

When book reporting gets "sticky" for your students, try this idea to explain how characters get into and out of "jams" or how they "preserve" things in their lives.

DIRECTIONS

1. Reproduce the cover page and lined jam jar page (pages 51 and 52) in quantities to meet the needs of the class. (The number of lined pages each student needs will vary.)

2. Reproduce page 54 for each student. Instruct the students to use any or all of the context clues to explain how characters in the chosen book get into "jams" or "preserve" things in their lives.

3. Have the students "cut out" the pages following the jam jar design and assemble the pages in the desired order with the cover page on top. The students may punch holes in the pages and tie them together with yarn.

4. Instruct each student to write his or her name on the first line of the cover page, the book title on the second line, and the author's name on the third line.

CONTEXT CLUES

1. _____ "spread the word" that
   _____ .

2. _____ was " in a jam" when
   _____ .

3. _____ "preserved" his/her dignity the time
   that _____ .

4. _____ felt like he/she was "spreading
   himself/herself thin" when _____ .

5. _____ "buttered up" _____
   when _____ .

6. _____ 's knees "turned to jelly" the time
   that _____ .

7. _____ thought that _____
   was "the berries" because _____ .

8. _____ felt "jammed up" because
   _____ .

JAM

All Sewed Up

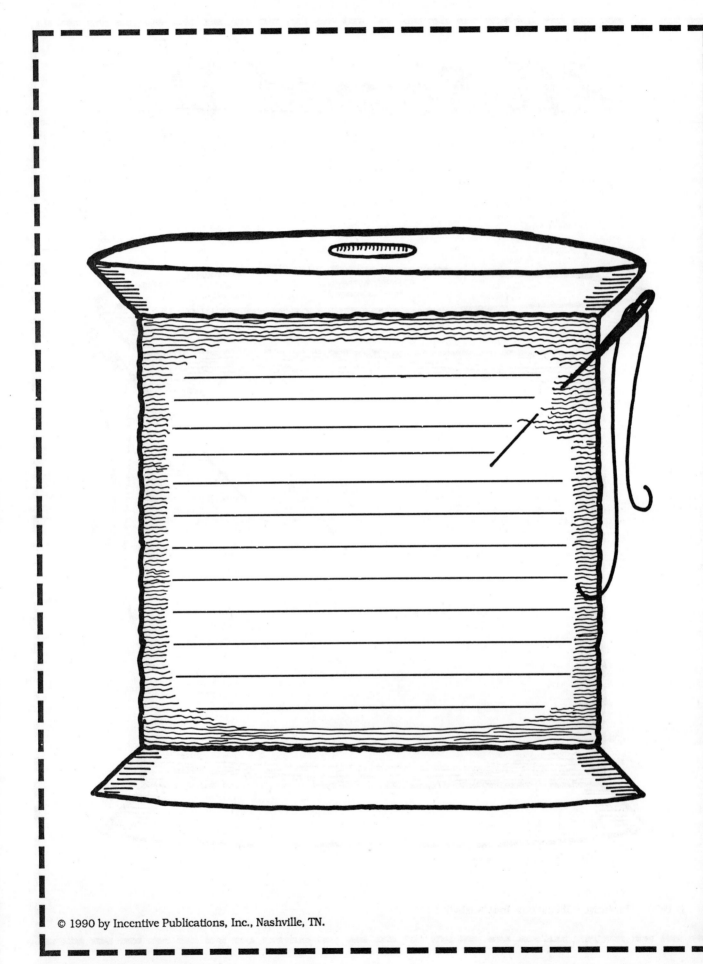

Are you tired of "threadbare" book reports? Your students will have good book reports "all sewed up" with this fun project!

DIRECTIONS

1. Reproduce the cover page and lined school page (pages 55 and 56) in quantities to meet the needs of the class. (The number of lined pages each student needs will vary.)

2. Reproduce page 58 for each student. Instruct the students to use any or all of the context clues to describe how the characters in the chosen book find themselves in dangerous situations and how they resolve their problems. The students also may describe dangerous events in the characters' lives.

3. Have the students "cut out" the pages following the spool design and assemble the pages in the desired order with the cover page on top. The students may punch holes in the pages and tie them together with yarn.

4. Instruct each student to write the book title on the first line of the cover page, the author's name on the second line, and his or her own name on the third line.

CONTEXT CLUES

1. _____ was kept "hanging by a thread" the time that _____ .

2. _____ thought that he/she had everything "all sewed up" when _____ .

3. When _____ happened, _____ was in "stiches."

4. _____ " came apart at the seams" when _____ .

5. _____ 's plans seemed to come "unraveled" after _____ .

6. It was like "looking for a needle in a haystack" when _____ tried to find/discover _____ .

7. _____ really "reaped what he/she sewed" after he/she _____ .

8. _____ was on "pins and needles" until _____ .

9. _____ made _____ so proud/excited, that he/she was about to "burst at the seams"!

forget *me *not

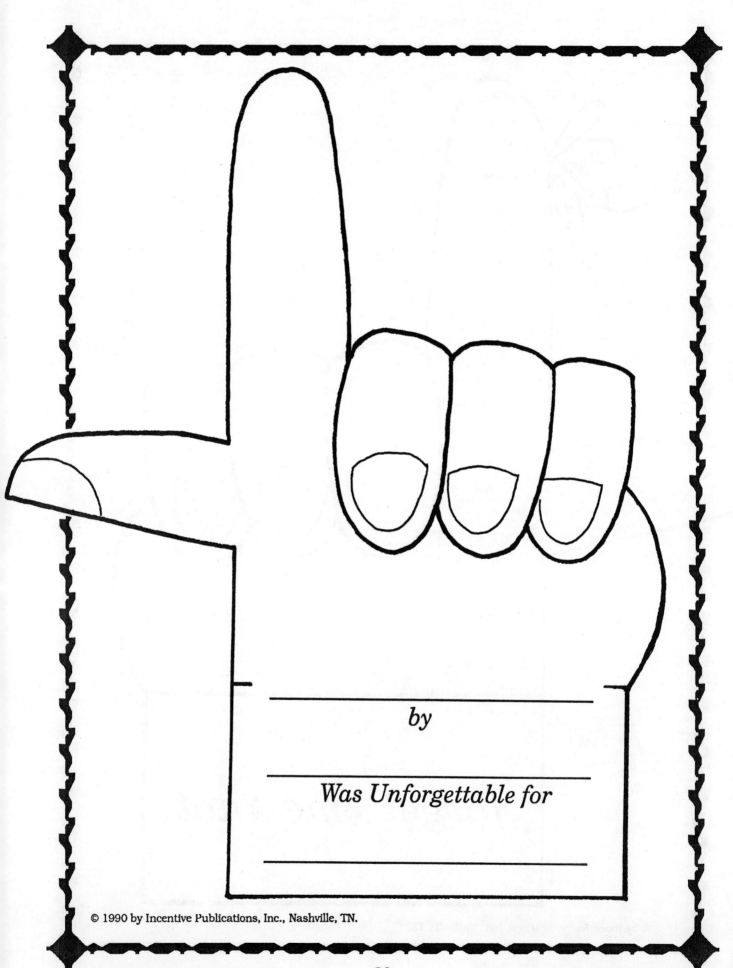

by

Was Unforgettable for

Can your students recall the last time they enjoyed book reporting? This "handy" idea will revive their memories of favorite books!

DIRECTIONS

1. Reproduce the hand patterns (pages 59-61) in quantities to meet the needs of the class. (Each student will need a lined page for each main character in the chosen book plus one additional lined page.)

2. Instruct the students to write the following on a lined hand page:
    *   what the character needed to remember, OR
    *   what the character forgot or should have forgotten, OR
    *   what happened as a result of the character's forgetfulness

3. Ask each student to decide if he or she would recommend the book to others. If so, the student should label a lined page "Give The Author A Hand"! and write about what makes the book unforgettable. If not, the student should label the page "On The Other Hand" and explain why the book should be forgotten.

4. Instruct each student to write the book title on the first line of page 60, the author's name on the second line, and his or her own name on the third line.

5. Have the students "cut out" the pages following the hand design and assemble them in the desired order with pages 59 and 60 on top (in that order) and the favorable or unfavorable "review" on the bottom. The students may punch holes in the pages and tie them together with yarn.

6. Have each student tie a string around the index finger of the cover page to tell others not to forget this book!

Just for the Record

Just for the record,

read

by

This fun activity will put students "on record" as readers of great books. Use this project to explain how book characters "record" special accomplishments.

DIRECTIONS

1. Reproduce the cover page and lined record page (pages 63 and 64) in quantities to meet the needs of the class. (The number of lined pages each student needs will vary.)

2. Reproduce page 66 for each student. Instruct the students to use any or all of the context clues to explain how the characters in the chosen book "go on record" for special achievements.

3. Have the students cut out the pages following the record design and assemble the pages in the desired order with the cover page on top. The students may punch holes in the pages and tie them together with yarn.

4. Instruct each student to write his or her name on the first line of the cover page (the curved line), the title of the book on the second line, and the author's name on the third line.

CONTEXT CLUES

1. _____ "went on record" as saying
   _____ when _____ .

2. _____ "set a record" for _____
   by _____ .

3. "For the record," _____ was
   _____ because _____ .

4. _____ was "in the groove" the time that
   _____ .

5. _____ went "round and round" with
   _____ about _____ .

6. It was "noteworthy" that _____ .

7. _____ told _____ , "off
   the record," that _____ .

8. _____ was "out of tune" with
   _____ because _____ .

9. It was "music to _____ 's ears" the time that
   _____ .

POINT THE WAY

DISCOVERED

BY

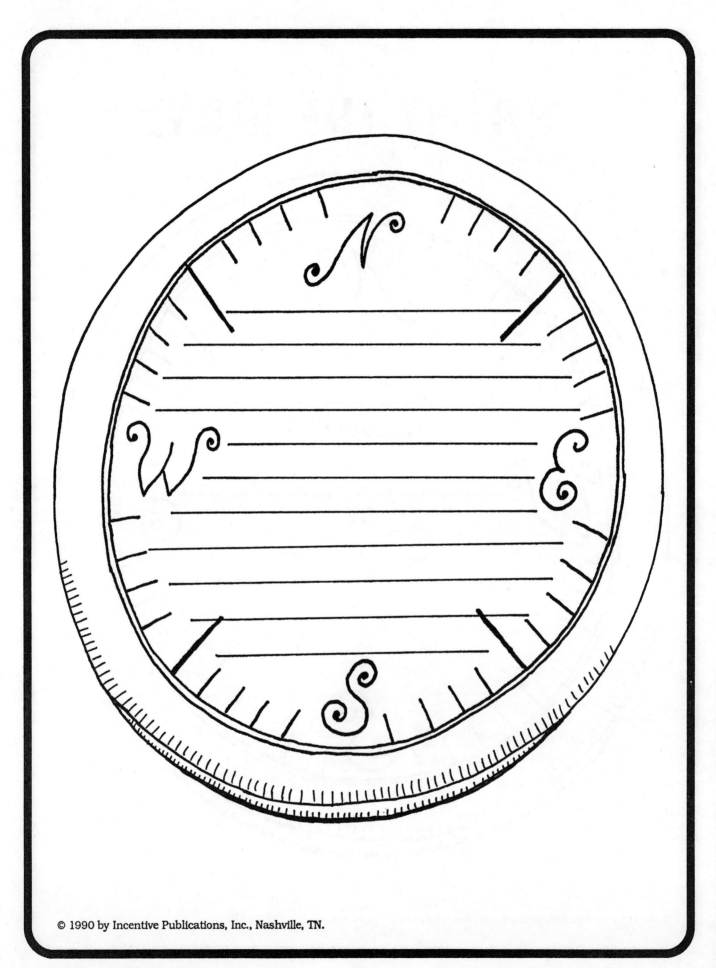

Here's a great book report project that will "point" students toward success. Your students will "explore" new territory as they explain how book characters need direction or find their way out of difficult situations.

DIRECTIONS

1. Reproduce the cover page and lined compass page (pages 67 and 68) in quantities to meet the needs of the class. (The number of lined pages each student needs will vary.)

2. Reproduce page 70 for each student. Instruct the students to use any or all of the context clues to explain how characters in the chosen book lack direction or find their way out of difficult situations.

3. Have the students "cut out" the pages following the compass design and assemble the pages in the desired order with the cover page on top. The students may punch holes in the pages and tie them together with yarn.

4. Instruct each student to write his or her name on the first line of the cover page, the book title on the second line, and the author's name on the third line.

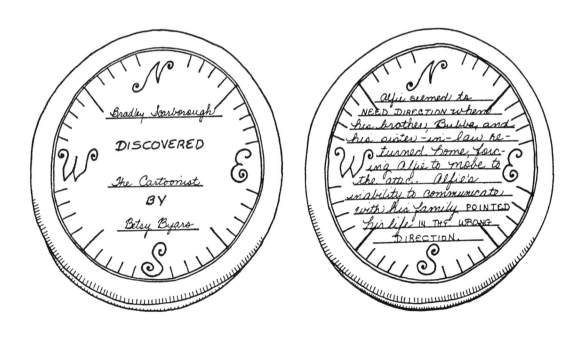

CONTEXT CLUES

1. _____ "needed direction"
when_____ .

2. _____ "pointed the way" to_____
after _____ .

3. _____ was "lost" after_____ .

4. _____ "knew his/her way around"
_____ .

5. _____ "followed in _____ 's
footsteps" when _____ .

6. _____ "hunted" for _____
because _____ .

7. _____ "searched his/her heart" about
_____ and found _____ .

8. _____ "lost sight
of"_____ the time that he/she
_____ .

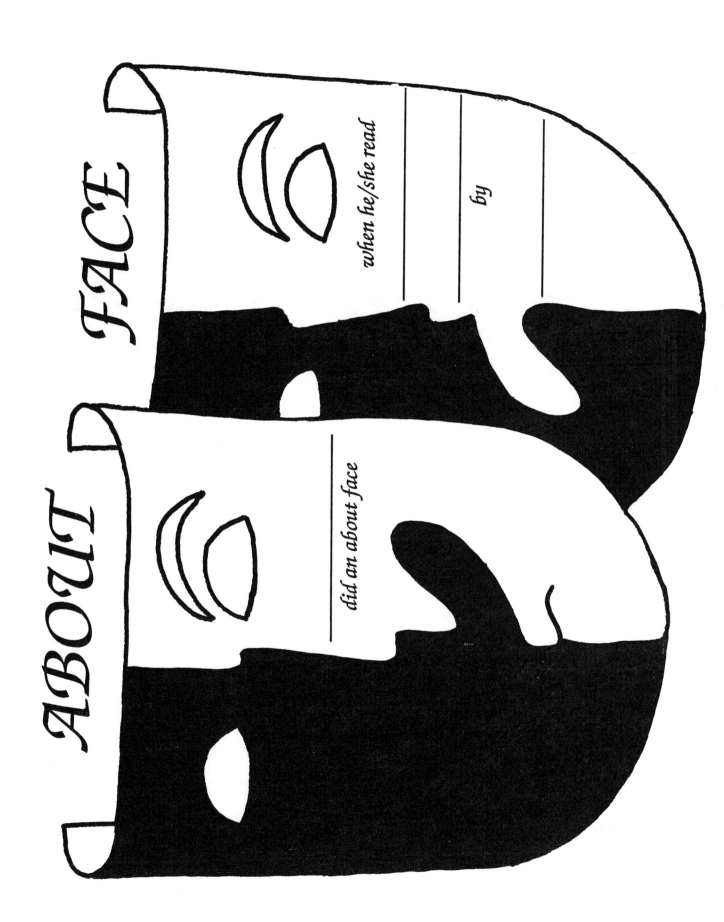

ABOUT FACE

when he/she read

by

did an about face

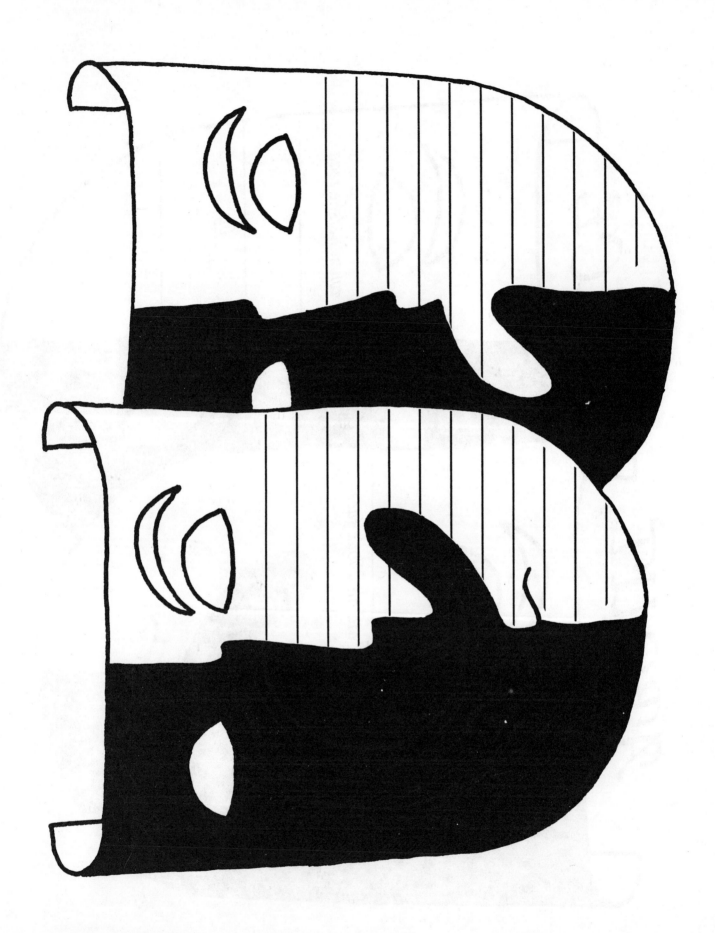

"Put a happy face" on book reporting! Have your students complete this project to compare and contrast characters and events.

DIRECTIONS

1. Reproduce the cover page and lined mask page (pages 71 and 72) in quantities to meet the needs of the class. (The number of lined pages each student needs will vary.)

2. Reproduce page 74 for each student. Instruct the students to use any or all of the context clues to compare or contrast book characters or their actions.

3. Have the students "cut out" the pages following the mask design and assemble the pages in the desired order with the cover page on top. The students may punch holes in the pages and tie them together with yarn.

4. Instruct each student to write his or her name on the line on the "comedy face" of the cover page and the book title and author's name on the lines on the "tragedy face."

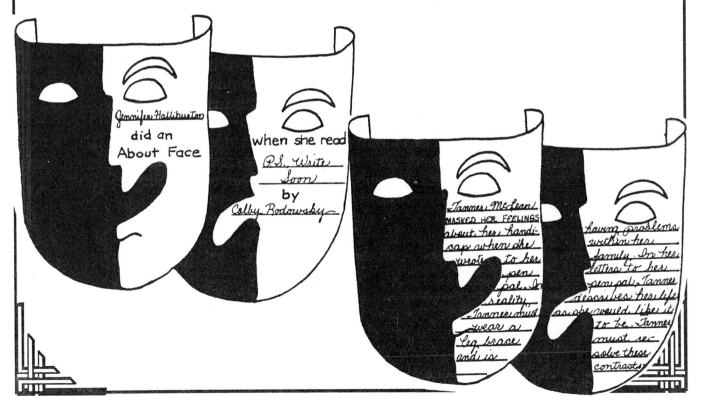

CONTEXT CLUES

1. _____ "masked" his/her feelings about _____ the time that _____ .

2. In "contrast" to _____ , _____ felt _____ about _____ .

3. It seemed like a "masquerade" to _____ when _____ .

4. _____ experienced "comic relief" when _____ .

5. It was "tragic" that _____ .

6. _____ was "upstaged" by_____ .

7. _____ "played a role" in _____ 's life.

8. _____ became "melodramatic" when _____ .

9. _____ became the "center of attention" when _____ .

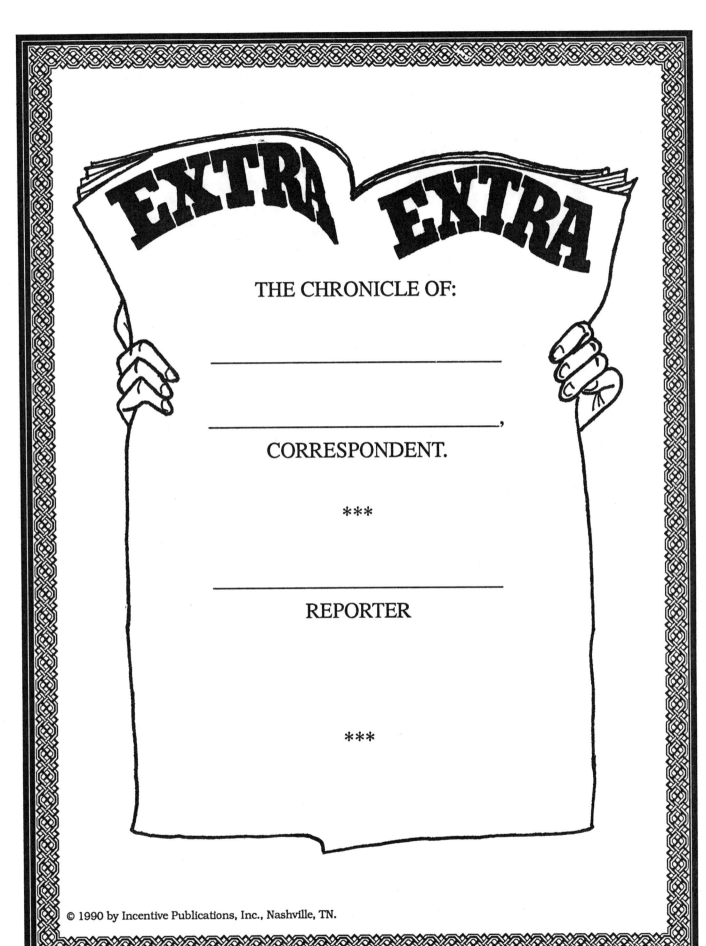

THE CHRONICLE OF:

_____

_____,

CORRESPONDENT.

***

_____

REPORTER

***

This "newsworthy" project will be a "headliner" for your students! Books with characters who deserve special recognition or who go the extra mile are perfect selections for this project.

DIRECTIONS

1. Reproduce the cover page and lined newspaper page (pages 75 and 76) in quantities to meet the needs of the class. (The number of lined pages each student needs will vary.)

2. Instruct each student to describe how the characters in the chosen book are important or how they "go the extra mile."

3. Have the students "cut out" the pages following the newspaper design and assemble them in the desired order with the cover page on top. The students may punch holes in the pages and tie them together with yarn.

4. Instruct each student to write the book title on the first line of the cover page, the author's name on the second line, and his or her own name on the third line (as the reporter).

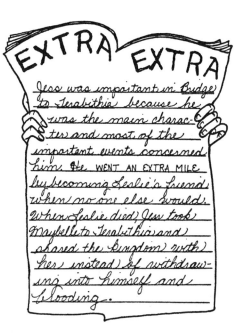

ON YOUR MARK!

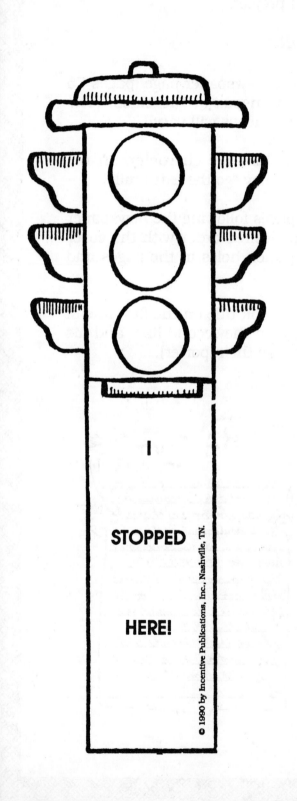

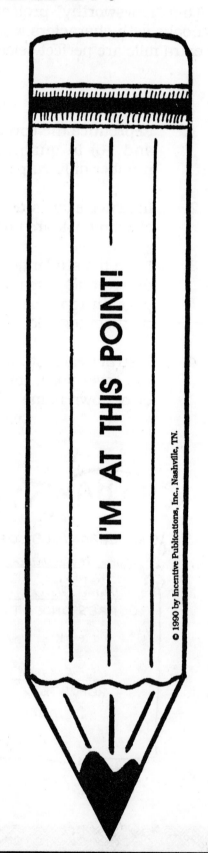

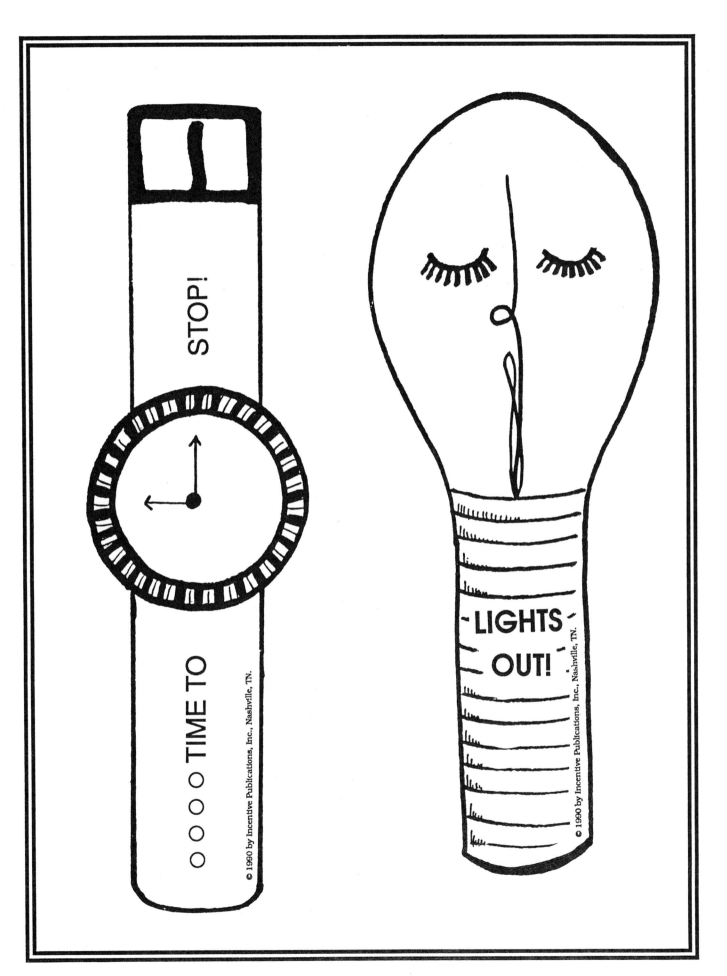